I ATE THE COSMOS FOR BREAKFAST

SAINT JULIAN PRESS

POETRY SERIES

Other Books by

Melissa Studdard

Six Weeks to Yehidah
My Yehidah: A Journal into the Story of You
The Tiferet Talk Interviews

I Ate the Cosmos
for Breakfast

Poems

by

Melissa Studdard

Saint Julian Press

Houston

Saint Julian Press, Inc.
2053 Cortlandt, Suite 200
Houston, Texas 77008
www.saintjulianpress.com

ISBN-13: 978-0-9889447-5-6
ISBN: 0-9889447-5-8
Library of Congress Control Number: 2014946724

Cover Art: *The Bravest Woman*
Size, 40 x 30
Oil On Canvas by Eric Anfinson.
Used by gracious permission of the artist.
www.ericanfinson.com

Author photo by Darren Trentacosta.
Post Production: Eve Harlowe
www.darrentrentacosta.com

Cover Design: Ron Starbuck

For Everyone Who Has Chosen Love Over Fear

Table of Contents

The poet is the priest of the invisible.
Wallace Stevens

I ATE THE COSMOS FOR BREAKFAST

I

Green shoot,
unfolding town of dark leaves,
birth my tiny, cosmic tongue.

CREATION MYTH

So there God lay, with her legs splayed,
birthing this screaming world

from her red velvet cleft, her thighs
cut holy with love

for all things, both big and small,
that crept from her womb like an army

of ants on a sugar-coated thoroughfare.
It wasn't just pebbles and boulders

and patches of sky, but the soul of sunlight,
the spirit of moon. She bore litters

of stars that glistened like puppies,
purring galaxies

robed in celestial fur, and galactic
clusters dusted with the scent of infinity.

It was her moment of victory:
the unveiling of seven billion milky breasts,

and she glowed—like a woman
in love with her own making, infatuated

with all corners of the blemished universe,
smitten with every imperfect thing:

splotchy, red-faced & wailing—
flawless in her omniscient eyes.

NIRVANA

—inspired by the Remedios Varo painting,
To Be Reborn

There's no mother's milk
the second time around,
just a crescent moon
floating in a goblet bigger
than your own head, or maybe
it's really the world in there,
shimmering and dark,
ready to be consumed.
I'd say be careful drinking
out of that thing, but
how trite it would sound
after what you've just
done, tearing through
Mother Earth's most intimate
fabric, ripping a frayed slit
for yourself. Think of trees
poking branches where
they don't belong,
encroaching windows built
to keep them out. You're
something like that, one
of nature's great mysteries
thrusting into the narrow rooms
of humanity, rattling
between the walls
of this synthetic
life, time after time, birth
after birth, like a hamster
in a cage on a wheel. Sure,
each ride is different, but
at some point you'll break
down that cage door, say
goodbye to the spinning
wheel, and finally run free.

IN ANOTHER DIMENSION, WE ARE MAKING LOVE

What color is dreaming? you ask.
I answer in the language of fleur-de-lis,
paisley and plaid. *Then, what is the sound of death?*
you ask, so I draw you a picture of dreaming.
What is left to know but that I'm re-writing the formula
for the air between us? Part nitrogen, part oxygen, the rest trace gasses
of love. Like you, I believe most in what
I cannot see or hear. Anger: a wounded steam
rising from the cauldron of your throat.
Alchemy: the steam dissipates, and you reach
across the table for my hand. So—
I note that it was already storming
before we arrived here, though my only proof
is an exhausted cloud passed out in the courtyard
and a thunderbolt curled up beside it.
I point out that in another dimension
this restaurant is a bedroom
in which we are making love. Don't
try to understand.
Just paint the air human,
take off your clothes,
hand back your coat of arms.
What you mistook for a person
is really a country
with a dark and sacred history
and no scholars to explain away the confusion.
Just burn the archives down.
Everything we have to know
we learned from a picture of dreaming.
Everything we need to remember
can fit on a scrap of paper
smaller than your hand.

EVEN THE LINGUIST GOES SILENT

The language of your thighs—
decapitated matches
still burning, decapitated verbs
spun loose, your body a woodshed
filled with nouns: goosedimple, cigarette
papers, stack of books in a corner
covered with web, ax with a broken handle.
I grab you there,
make something new, fire.
Make something new,
the wheel, make Twinkies,
a microwave—your colloquial
unfolding. I think you on my lips,
the galactic vocabulary of your kisses.
Make poems of your toes, make novellas
of how light visits your iris. Translate you
into me, transcribe the files—the softest part.
What you told me
is true: In passion, the linguist
goes silent. New galaxies
swarm like gnats,
spin on the startled tongue.

TITHING

—for Hildegard of Bingen

In my dreams I speak the language of your visions,
lingua ignota of the milky sky. This earth was made

to nurture us, the clouds to quench, the trees
and flowers to bloom your alphabet: *Scivias*,

Liber vitae meritorum, De operatione Dei—
bursts of fuchsia light, petals of divinity

unfolding in your eye, the open arms of God
ushering in the healing waters of the Rhine.

You held the chalice high, took your sips
from every inch of the rim,

fed them back to us, pre-digested, lit
from within the golden beak of illumination,

glowing inside the ruby lungs of your canticles.
In the dreams I am your Jutta, your Volmar,

your confessor, your scribe. You are the tithe
to the world from our cloistered realm;

you are the tithe to above from a bankrupt world;
you are the ten per cent that earns our human keep.

I ATE THE COSMOS FOR BREAKFAST

—after Thich Nhat Hanh

It looked like a pancake,
but it was creation flattened out—
the fist of God on a head of wheat,
milk, the unborn child of an unsuspecting
chicken—all beaten to batter
and drizzled into a pan.
I brewed some tea and closed my eyes
while I ate the sun, the air, the rain,
photosynthesis on a plate.
I ate the time it took that chicken
to bear and lay her egg
and the energy a cow takes
to lactate a cup of milk.
I thought of the farmers, the truck drivers,
the grocers, the people
who made the bag that stored the wheat,
and my labor over the stove seemed short,
and the pancake tasted good,
and I was thankful.

II

Robe to the floor,
moon inventing skin, slant
of silver, shaped like you.

NAMING SKY

This sky is a lovemaking—tangerine fire
with bridges of cloud, the spread legs

of the poplar grove, open to all that is blue.
Here, someone has built a temple

of a drift of wind, where mallards and grouse
worship time's forgotten mouth—

shape me like a kiss beneath this sky.
My hands are blossoms, fine mists. My heart

is a rowboat, rocking in green waves.
My thoughts are birch leaves, carried on a waft,

holy with the work of light through a dapple
of aphid bites. Would it be okay if I called this God?

If I pointed out how clouds have begun to undress
the mountain? There are bridges

inside minutes, towers inside hours, windows
at the edge of day. The months swim

with a slow precision into years, and always,
the sky keeps being the sky. And this God we love

stays too naked to wear skin. See the tangle
she's made of her limbs? Her right leg is a riverbank,

and her left, the start and end of night.
Her arms are the tides that pull and push you out again.

Kneel to the temple of wind. Listen to the voices
lingering in trees. When they moan,

it is your name they call. You can answer
with touch. You can call them God or sky or self.

You can carry them with you
when you row your sunset back home.

WE ARE THE UNIVERSE

—inspired by the Eric Anfinson painting,
The Bravest Woman

Watching your mouth as you eat I think
perhaps an apple is the universe and your body
is an orchard full of trees. I've seen the way your leaves
cling to the ground in fall, and I noticed then
that your voice sounded soft, like feathered, drifting things
coming finally to rest. Note:
I was the core in your pink flesh. You
were hungry birds
and foxes walking though the miles of me.
You climbed, dug your nails in my bark, yanked
something loose. Don't tell me what it is.
Just keep it close.
Because I planted these rows
and rows of myself for you—
so I could lick the juice from your lips,
so I could remember
how round and hot
the promise of seed. If I could find
that orchard right now, I'd run all through the rows
of you. I'd stand in the center and twirl
until, dizzy, I fell. I'd climb high and shake
until the only thing left in you was longing,
and you'd write a poem for me. You'd say:
Your mouth is the universe. Your desire
is an orchard full of trees.

WHEN YOU DO THAT

It feels like millions of tiny
harps are playing inside my body
and all the extinct animals
that ever were
are again
running into you
inside me
their hooves and claws
burning on the unexpected
asphalt
their tongues alive
with the ministry of light

FOR TWO CONVERSION THERAPISTS WHO FELL IN LOVE AND BECAME GAY ACTIVISTS

Sometimes God holds up a mirror full of fate
and you find yourself in a King-bed room in a one-hotel
town, with *No Vacancy* flashing amber epiphanies
across each other's eyes. Train yourself then to bear
witness to divine love. The infinite grace. The ultimate
knowing. You've heard it said God sleeps in the stone,
dances in the kindling's split stick. But who
knew she also rustled among cheap white sheets?
Don't put a black light on those things.
What came before doesn't matter. Listen to grace
in the coffeemaker's drip, in the crying infant next door,
in the annoying whirr of the window unit blowing air.
Listen when God knocks on the door in the morning
and says, *I brought you a paper, some orange juice,
and two Eden-colored plums.* The truth is
God is sprawled naked across the sky. The truth is
God runs the bordello inside your heart. It's full
of all life's misfits you tried to hide: the mullet
and skinny legs, the letters you wrote to the man
next door but never sent, your secret affinity
for reality TV. Make love to every luscious thing
you find there. Your atoms have come to worship
and rejoice at the temple of the familiar.

THE SHEPHERD OF HAPPENSTANCE

I was a gypsy with hips like prophesy
and sandstorms in my eyes.
       Oh Lordy,
seventeen husbands and two-hundred children.
I traveled so far,
     drank so much wine.
My feet were the keys of pianos, playing
miles and miles of sand.
       No lie,
I meant to build a camp and stay moonstruck,
near the cave,
     to dance through the night.
Why didn't I just go inside the trumpet's lip
and stay? I carried a continent on my back,
      a sack of sea.
Mother of God. Did you hear the prophecy? Conformity,
conformity, conformity.
      And plans for escape.
Broke a lot of laws. But remained their plastic doll,
small-waisted, full of lip & shine.
      Father,
they drowned me at the bottom of a river
in a dress made of rocks.
      Sang a lot of songs.
I've always longed for the forest at night, the sounds,
the owls.
     Great spirit,
I was a wisp of steam on a lake that no one saw.
      Oh Lordy.
Bless me. End me. Save me.
I've traveled so long.

III

Lavender & rose—
Oh, how we paint these dreams
blooming into light.

LOOKING AT *A YOUNG WOMAN*
WITH A WATER JUG

Can you see the way Vermeer
twirls light
around his thumb,
pulls it straight again
and lays it across a vase
or table—

how the instant
between a smile
and a smile expired
can be brought to focus
with color?

No more
are shadows hid in dark
but something felt
in sanguine or cobalt—
a cold shimmer
at the rim of a golden jug,

as if friction
between objects
required only nearness,
as if a pale, blue drape
had kindness to give
to a brass wash basin.

Our human minds
are like these objects—
delivering and seeking
the same light
from different points,
casting radiant shadows
on other minds,

like some swart alchemy
brewing in a basement lab,
the commingling of hues
in a cast-iron pot,
and the rising of mind
laid bare on mind,
the rising of pure idea.

STARRY NIGHT, WITH SOCKS

Neruda eats gates and barbed wire, absorbs the nails
and exhales a borderless world—language that
skips and spins across the ground of flight, syntax
that never learned what it can't do, so does.
Van Gogh sees the aura of night. Saw the aura of chair.
Of desk. Pipe. Saw thick swirls of angst and relief in the sky,
everything pulsing and alive, vibrant with being: the skirt
swish of a spiral galaxy, the cypress fingers' reach,
space-time splayed with light and steeple,
with neurons firing into the curve of line, a synaptic
dance between canvas and paint, landscape and ode.
From the poet's mouth, by the painter's hand:
Simple strokes lead to love.
And know now what Neruda saw: A sock can be
the microcosm of all things good, knitted by Mara Mori,
with glowing strands of twilight and thread,
holy as a sacred text
placed on that great altar, the foot.
Because things are not things alone. They are also
that which made them. A sock is a little, woolen god.
It is a woman stopping by with a gift. It is the warmth of two
hands rubbed together,
a fire cradling your heels and soles.

EVERYTHING IS SO DELICIOUS

Sometimes
I feel so hungry, so thirsty,
I don't want to die.
This desire to butter and eat the stars.
This desire to pack the sunset in my bag
and run home with her, to make
a terrarium for the moon.
You see, a pirouette
once courted a flying leap.
Rim of day
married the indispensability of night,
and from these, my parents
were born, half-human, half-dream,
unafraid of madness, desperation, delight,
weavers of magic,
gifted with the ability
to bend and reshape
time. That's why
if I climb a tree I can find
the top of myself.
If I dig up the garden,
galaxies start seeding there.
Look at this bloom of world,
this unfurling universe
drifting to rest on my tongue.
Even the mud is prime
for making pies—and the chopped up
meaty bits of sky, and the salted ocean.
And the life in me—
the life in me so piquant and sweet—
I've claimed my banquet
from the ether
and I'm never letting go.

A GARDEN FOR AMYTIS

Be still. The Hanging Gardens were a dream
That over Persian roses flew to kiss
—Trumbull Strickney

Nebuchadnezzar II knew woman
by her real name:
flower, fountain, dewdrop.
He knew that to win her
even in the desert
was not impossible,
because
if his imagination was moist
and his heart was like soil,
he could become more
than mere conqueror—
he could be a creator too,
and he would grow not only roses
or dangling fragrant vines,
but there in Babylon
he could grow, also,
that hardiest of stalks:
love.

PAINTING YOU INTO THE SCENE

Because the sun hangs in the sky like a small, folded hand,
I count the brush strokes leading into evening. There are

so many ways to bathe a night in darkness, to wrap the indigo
of memory around a porch swing, to place a hound dog

like a river of mercy at someone's feet. Because the dog's
foot twitches when he is dreaming, I paint a chapel in the distance,

and people spilling down a tulip-dotted hill. I paint
their laughter, that forgiveness, into the flicker of a street lamp,

its yellow pulse a perfect passage home. There are so many
ways to paint *I miss you*—to show your letter, resting

on a chair, to place your tea cup, steaming, beside a plate
of toast, as if by committing color to canvas, I could draw you

here to me forever. Because the teacup sits next to a window,
I paint a blue jay plying its nest, I paint a hornet, I paint

a schoolgirl jumping rope. And because the letter says
I'm coming back to you I fold the night into darkness,

tuck the sun between indigo sheets, and study recipes for mixing
skin tones—a little ochre, some burnt sienna, some desire.

IV

Under an old mat
overgrown by weeds,
the key I cannot find.

WHERE THE GATEKEEPER LIVES

Inside you, there's a gatekeeper
with all the keys.
There's a summer morning
shaped like a woman's throat.
There's something you wanted
to say:
that to unlock suffering
is to acknowledge death,
that death is the color of deep waters,
of miso and seaweed, of eyes
dilated by lust.
Inside you, a cactus
bursts with a thousand golden fruits.
The gatekeeper opens a lock,
peels a rind.
There are so many things you want
to do. You're a bloom of bones
and sacred blood. You're the one whose sleep
throws itself into rivers
waiting to be born,
the one whose fear scales mountains
when it could be picking locks.
Inside you, there's a shipwreck
and survivors
swimming towards the shore.
Inside you,
a sleight of self
still tries to open the doors.

OM

She sent us flowers without a card,
God did—that trickster soul.
It must have been a sound that started it all,
and she's still out there somewhere, laughing
while we seek directions, or direction,
while we, the addressees, search for an addresser,
while we sort and sift and categorize and collect,
divide, classify and analyze. Our refrigerators hum to us,
and heaven knows the bugs make merry at night.
Once I even saw yellow hum
when I imagined Van Gogh stroking its thick,
vibrancy onto the page.
That yellow was anything but hum-drum.
I swear, I felt it on the roof of my mouth
and at the back of my throat,
a yogic ritual or some sort of Tantric stunt.
Even deep in my chest, yes, I felt the hum.
And in the other room—the clothes in the washer,
round and round they went, a spinning universe,
and next to them, a parallel world, the dryer,
connected by the same outlet,
humming away.
This life is anything but ho-hum,
with all this motion and noise.
Hell, I can hardly hear over the buzz of my phone,
which I have cursed for interference,
which I have indignantly nicknamed,
that silver piece of shit,
which I have threatened to replace (like it cares),
and which was really Om all along.
Washing clothes, I've since learned, is an act of prayer.

SUDDEN ENCOUNTERS

—inspired by the Remedios Varo painting,
Exploration of the Source of the Orinoco River

The Orinoco overflows from a goblet,
spouts from the center as though
water had wings. I'm telling you,
this goblet rests on a table
in the hollow of a tree—so
deliberate you can't help
but question if the almighty
watchmaker set it there herself.
Paley would have had his say,
to be sure, but this is about Varo
and her own fantastical teleology,
about how the source is never
what you would expect, how
inspiration is a pink dolphin
swimming through the rivers of night,
daring you to look into its eyes, to chance
a lifetime of nightmares
for the purchase of a moment of genius,
to be the woman manning a vessel
no one has ever seen, like Varo
herself—skating the surface
with wings, her retinas burnt and open
by frequent, sudden encounters
with dark and unholy gods.

NO PHILOSOPHER HAS YET SOLVED
THE PROBLEM OF EVIL

I guess the sunset forgot to tell them about its beauty.
Ditto the stars.
Because the evening smells
like gun smoke. And someone's down,
or passed out. Too much whistling and
forgot to take a breath. No. Look
how beautiful, the night—
dusk cracked
open and growing a strange silence,
blood on the floor
worm in the blood,
body clinging to the soul like a parasite.
I don't have to say it. You know what I mean.
What I'm asking. Why?
Didn't they see the sunset?
Didn't they see the stars?

INTEGRATING THE SHADOW

I was a bird in the hand of God.

I was two in the bush,

the yin to my own yang, yang to yin,
drinking gin on the porch at midnight,
or otherwise drinking tea—you see

how it is—Bach on Tuesdays—Thursdays
acid rock, tie-dyed t-shirts and jeans.
Mornings I fed the needy and blessed
their souls with sticky kisses.
I sang to them and lotioned their feet
with lilac cream and peppermint oil,
humbled by their poverty, inspired
by the way they got out of bed
without cigarettes or coffee.
Afternoons I cursed their lazy
asses and stepped over them
in the streets on my way to the pub
seeking a little warmth or a quiet corner
in which to ponder the implication
of lips on brass, to dance, unmolested,
with my own shadow, which was my worst
enemy, and, conspicuously, my only friend.

I was a bird in the hand of God.

I was two in the bush.

I was a pair of white pants in a drive-by
puddle splash, a drunk with beer down
the front of my shirt. I was ketchup
on my own sleeve, a rash on an otherwise
clear face, a tainted, defiled disaster,
stained by life, soiled and damn near effaced
by that often unrecognizable prankster,
my troublemaker, my doppelganger,
that saucy vamp, grace.

VAGABOND

Again at the precipice
we stood, a torrent of wind,
a rainstorm of love, a dark
& brooding lick of thunder.
Just one slip of the foot
and our gypsy hearts would be
rolling again. While the others
made babies, we birthed the jagged
edges of cliffs, the imperceptible
blue of sky, the spokes of caravan,
swaddled it all in chainmail,
and left it there to fend for itself—
a modern bond, held but not nurtured,
cherished but not maintained. You
dressed me in bells like a cat, and when
I danced, you dropped scarlet
and lilac scarves at my feet,
you doused me in the thick sweat
of wine, stained me henna
with your rough and unread palms,
and I loved you the only way my nomad
lips could, like a plectrum kissing
a lyre, strumming dust up from silence
as often and as long
as I could coax rainstorms out of song.

IF I SAW THE AIRPORTS IN YOUR EYES

& if I saw the planes
coming and going, if I saw
your packed bags on the trolley
to Terminal A

I'd be the city
with my long neck stretched back.
I'd be a tall building burning down.
I'd climb into winter and shut the lid,
pack myself tight like brown sugar
pressed with a spoon.
I'd say *don't remind me.*
Please don't remind me.

But it's too late
because it's snowing
in all the counties of my body,
and the tarmac is slick with quiet,
and the exhaust of you
punches through my sky
like a fist.

VI

With feathers, the thing
with feathers, emerging lopsided
from the clouds.

BAREBACK ALCHEMY

Bring on the cold.
I'm going to meet this life
without gloves or scarves or boots
and ride bareback through the cobbled
sweeps of street, howling incantations
into mist and threading mystery
through the folds of day. Let the ticking
minutes land where they may:
I point my heart at uncharted
paths, lift from the earth,
trot on the wind. No Nostradamus
could predict the twists and turns
this horse will take
down alleys and through storms,
her divining tail,
her Medusa mane—
how she clops the cobblestone
and tries, tries like hell
to buck me off. Let it
snow and sleet. I've got no fur
coat to meet winter with this year,
just a raw and broken heart
and the waterfalls in my chest
where my lungs used to be.
So go ahead. Bring it on: fire
and ice, hurricanes, tsunamis, quakes.
I've got the freedom of the dispossessed,
that tornado in my throat,
the lick of truth,
and I'll sing it loud.
I'll wear the philosopher's stone
like a smile, don a raven
on my shoulder, conjure the alchemy
to twist my demons into gods.

THE DREAM

A great soft arm
reaches down from the sky,

turned up for me to climb.
I dance in the palm,

shimmy my way up, heel
a little jig, and drop to curtsey

before two huge eyes,
open as a schoolhouse

airing itself out, its dusk echo
beckoning the past. Yes,

I remember this. Tetherball,
hopscotch, my pet rock Sally.

When I lost her, I cried.
Same when I skinned my knee,

killed my favorite frog. See me
there—child of heartache

and tangled vines, tall forts
and trampolines—taming whole

universes with my star-tipped wand.
The seats of my swing set—

cushions on thrones.
What do I hope for now

that I couldn't imagine then?
I might stretch my own

great arm, smudge
these fingertips with dream stuff,

and turn my palm up to everything
that wants to dance with me.

SUBTERRANEAN

I'm not talking about the underside of a kitten's
belly, or the layers of dress on a modest woman's

corpse. I don't mean that beneath the skin there's
a world of vein, meat and bone. No, I'm talking about

mantle and core—the viscous, shifting substrata
beneath the camel's hoof, beneath the sand,

beneath the crust beneath the sand. I think there are
birds in there, flying around inside the earth's body,

birds flying over oceans, streams and lakes, children
laughing beside rivers, mothers calling them home

to supper by beating wooden spoons on the sides
of aluminum pots. It doesn't matter that we can't see

them, or even that my theory has been disproven.
I go where the laughter is, pure and simple, and I say

this ball of clay is really an onion, a snake coiled
around a bouncing ball, a swirl of petals exploding

from bud. It's simple, really: Love is the pack on a
hitchhiker's back, everything he owns, everywhere

he goes, the only article that can't be left behind.
And we've all got our thumbs out, pointed towards

that other realm, the one beneath the skin, beneath
the bone and marrow and veiny streams of blood, where gods

await us like lovers, like dense smoke, like cracked
and forgotten mirrors, reflecting the singular route home.

DAUGHTER

—for Rosalind

Because I was a cave,
and you were the bird that flew through
my hollows, when they bathed the pain away,
the light on your face looked like
peace after a long and onerous
war. I knew then what it meant
to conjure fire
from two sticks, to be an ocean
giving life to a wave, to invent
the wheel and its axle, unwind torque,
create a perfect language
from gurgles and sighs. Your body
was a new and sacred space. I was a universe
cooling after a great expanse.
And because bright cells
clung together to be you,
I could believe
I built the ark that saved humanity.
In animals walking two by two.
That I'm the one who sat beneath
the Bodhi tree
and begot the sacred fig
of enlightenment.
I tell you, Athena sprung
from my own split
head. Because
emergence is a teaching.
Because your hands and feet
were softer than sand. Because before
there were canyons
or valleys or lakes or winds,
you curled your hand around my finger,
and, with your touch, delivered the all.

FOR THE WOMEN OF ATENCO

Take it now, this metaphor, your bread.
You've seen God bleeding in the streets,
but the militia couldn't help, sooty faced
themselves, disoriented by the shrapnel
lodged beneath their right to choose
a peaceful life. Take these words flowing
like wine. Let them salve where hands
gripped too tight, where teeth broke the skin,
where fists beat your notions of freedom
and equality flat as powdered dough, flat
as grapes crushed beneath the pointed
boots of war. Let these words recall
those things you meant to be before
rage came storming through your town.
Let them be your appetizers,
served to you with the humility and respect
you were denied four years ago.
Let these words be your dinners and desserts,
evidence you are being heard. Let them
sustain you, as others sip margaritas on the patio,
as others go on about their lives
oblivious to what you have endured. Your time
will come. So keep your aprons on, women
of Atenco; keep your eyes on the timer
and your hearts on the cause—because grapes
beneath the feet become wine, and
dough that is set aside will rise. Yes—
neglected, resilient dough will rise.

I FELL IN LOVE WITH A DOUBLE-YOLK EGG

In the egg
that cracked its head,
a tree and butterfly were dancing,
yellow wings, yellow leaves,
yellow, yellow—
breaking away from trunk. Who
painted all that yellow in there?
I'm falling in love with movement,
the swirl of yolk, a sapling hand
on the butterfly's back, a spin, a dip,
the swish of nucleus
flying into the rafters of bowl,
and here comes my lovemaking
hand, wanting to hold it all together:
how the egg and milk marry bread,
dressed in a dash of cinnamon.
Exotic, scented gown.
Polygamous ritual.
Eyes like ovenlight.
I disappeared into it all,
skipped across the rim of shell,
forgot my name and where I came from.
Hadn't I been to the source and back?
When they found me, I was dancing with apples
next to the handle of a floured pin.

VII

When the dream forgets
to end itself, you will know
you are not asleep.

THEY WHO SEE IN THE DARK

—for Noor Basra and Noor Sheza,
two girls murdered for dancing in the rain

So freedom would rain
in the ballrooms of their chests,
they entered sideways through the pulse
of hands on imaginary drums. One
wore a wing beat in her eye,
the other, groves of laughter in her thumbs,
and all the while, they called it dancing.
You should have seen the way
they gathered nightfall into song.
To stretch their necks.
Their covered heads. To paint their deaths
as rainbows after someone else's storm.
Who would guess clipped wings could
sissonne high enough to fly—
that each giggle, every spin,
would be a prelude to bullets singing
hate to hollow bones? In their town, clouds
were gaunt countries, begging
exiles into tombs. So, to show respect—
leave the dead unburied.
An opera of bitter winds
will come to honor life.

I DREAM; THEREFORE YOU ARE

Moon & Pillow
say this is yesterday, and I've
pasted you back together
with salt. I mixed you with straw
& carried you into the desert to dry. My adobe
tulip,
                        my red earth, my paper doll,
I forgot that the rock I propped
you up against
was made of tombstone,
so I searched beneath your eyelids
for an explanation of color. I built
highways & colonies across
the meadows of sleep.
I followed you into the temple of absence
to learn how to die.
                Don't you know
how hard it is to keep you
buried? *Please.*
                    Have some compassion.
It's like a swamp in this desert.
The caskets are at sea level
and always rising. See—
there you go, floating by, mouth full of
music and death.
I guess this means they finally told you:
You are the corpse in this off-key song.
And my words are a pilgrimage
bearing gifts. I brought you flowers.
Is it too late? Are you hungry?
I'm planting a casserole
in the grass.

KILLING THE MOTH

Yesterday I drew a very big, rather rare night moth, called the death's head, its colouring of amazing distinction . . . I had to kill it to paint it, and it was a pity, the beastie was so beautiful. —*Vincent Van Gogh*

The flapping of night-wings by fire,
a rattling in the skull,
a moth, wings cloudy white,
tinged carmine and faded green:
all is captured in a sigh of pity—
beauty must hold still to be seen.

What is death to the dead
when art gives wing to the living?
When what was gauzy and frail
presses its form to human
shores, to be held there, foam swept
through quicksilver days,
there to withstand the turning of seasons.

The leaves will green again,
brown again, gold, and green again.
The leaves will go red.
Red, and the death's head moth flutters,
steadfast, swept beyond the joy and danger
of a shift in wind.

Artist, have you learned the moth?
You are more alike than you can see.
Not in the way a night can swarm to flame,
but like a gust of stars
breathless with foretelling—

Markings, like the lines
that streak your palm, tell of leaves
pressed into a book. Their color fades.
They rot. They leave behind
an imprint on the page.

YOU WERE A BIRD; YOU ARE THE SEA

—inspired by the John Sokol painting,
Icarus Practicing

Stretch them wide
as God's first breath.

From tip to tip
there is no time.

Just the rumbling
of a tune

in your makeshift
beak, and bright

sky galloping
through the hollow

of bone. Bucket
of air, spine built

from light, boy
full of flutters

and drafts—you
speak mountain

stream, laurel leaf,
rolling cloud—

the dialect of flight.
The world drifts

like a madness
inside you—earth,

trees, and birds,
feathers, wings,

and night, the start
and end of time

rowing through
blood's currents,

sailing inside
the freedom

of mind,
now split open

by a whirlwind
of koan, pushed

like air through
sky's vast lung.

When I go,
let me go

like you, Icarus,
past my own

limits before
I fall. Let me

be a flesh-toned
streak in the sky,

a flash in the blue,
a sunburst

of wonder
rejoining

the ripples
of sea.

FOR BAUDELAIRE

In the woods you found a carcass with maggots in its chest,
with waterfalls in its eyes, with the buzz of life still

hovering around its skull, and in commemoration, you grabbed
your sweetheart's hand, with your left, and on your right, you

snatched the clasped hand of the world and said: Look here, how
we build skyscrapers in the cavity of death's groin, how we

paint lilacs on its ribs. We will drive motor cars over its
bones and laugh in the waning perfume of midnight, and, my love,

I will write you a poem, a tribute to your beautiful decay,
to your rotting thighs, to the death you will birth with sex

because, truly, this is beauty—this festering carcass in the woods,
this putrid nag, truth. And in it, you will live forever.

VIII

Green shoot, birth of worlds,
unfolding town of dark leaves:
All is new again.

BAREFOOT RONDELET

—inspired by the Remedios Varo painting,
To Be Reborn

To be reborn,
step barefoot from this world, praying
to be reborn
wild-eyed, seared by life, and graying
already with wisdom, forewarned:
it's a sad, sweet, brief delaying,
to be reborn.

A PRAYER

Someday I'll meet you again,
and we'll sleep like the eyes of hurricanes,
lidless in our trek to taste each other's tongues
as they throw dirt over my face, into the quivers
of my throat. I've been meaning to say a little
something each night, to light a candle
in the doorframe, set fire
to the empty church: For you, I'd drive
the people back into each other's arms,
where they could see, finally, your
softness again. I meant to say I knew you
were unhoused, the original nomad. There were
none living there among the pews. What was left
was pressed among the pages of psalmody.
And this is no new thing.
Another costume off: My golden hair.
My blue-green eyes.
Shed beneath the dirt.
I meant to say, *how are you?* And, also,
this is not about me. Because there are tigers
scratching at the swirling wind, and there are monsters
banging on the shutter doors. Because I've had no time
to think or eat properly or rest.
It was all just a blind sneeze in the wind.
Let me know everything about you, please.
I'll go back. Do it right this time.
I'll be a dragonfly, a pebble, an earthworm, a flea.

KISS THE WORLD WITH MY WOUNDED MOUTH

This heart I wear on my sleeve
is a dowry. I will marry
the scent of cherry blossoms drifting
down in a swirl. I will marry the moment
anger transforms into forgiveness.
I will marry that wild animal,
my own body, and take up residence
inside the thatched hut
of my soul. Look
how I make love to the reach of light
angling in from the east, to the sound of hooves
on hard ground, to the ground itself.
See how I embrace
the jostle of water
sloshing against the side of a boat.
Nothing can stop me
from offering my own exploding
heart from my two hands. Nothing
can stop me
from trespassing
through the weedy and nettled
plots of love.

IF ONLY FOR THE SAKE OF BLOOMING

When I saw you walk across the lake
I opened an enchanted door and got out my magic
canoe to follow. I could hear
laughter coming from the buoys and motorboats
and jetskis and oars. My own oars! Laughing!
Calling out, *Looser, Looser, you're out of your league*—
even though
I'd held them so firmly in my hands.
To begin with, I am
dead—dead liver, dead hair,
dead mouth. Cat's had my tongue for at least
a week, and when I stopped by the graveyard
to pay my respects, they put an urn around my head.
They hung me at the end of my rope by my toes.
I thought it was over—the war, the suffering,
the ridiculous joy, the nights of wine and lovemaking—
But I broke loose, and now I stand with a clump
of you in my hand. Lover. Dark soil.
Deadhead my remains and reap
again. I am that Bloodhound pacing the shore—
a scrap of nightshirt in my teeth and your story
on my tongue. The Dogwood that fell—
was it a fable? How the tree didn't understand endings?
The rot and flourish? The procession
of petal? The green dirge?
I am that tree
and something has burrowed inside my hollow.
See how I love? Like a mother
hosting the body that steals residence.
Like a lover
uprooted at the shore.
I'll grab my mocking canoe and smartass
oars and row. I'll lean my dead self to the ground
and bloom.

THE SOUL IS SWADDLED IN BODY

If I could do it all over again,
I wouldn't write a damn word. I'd
just make love to you in the meadow
with the cows watching, and the cats
chasing mice through the straw.

ACKNOWLEGEMENTS

I extend my deepest gratitude to the editors and staff members of the following journals, magazines, and anthologies in which poems from this collection have appeared or will soon appear: *Anthology of Muse for Women, Beat Texas Anthology, Boulevard, Connecticut Review, Control Literary Magazine, The Crafty Poet, The Criterion, Dash Literary Journal, di-vêrsé-city, Edgar Allen Poet Journal, The Fox Chase Review, Free Poetry, The Great American Poetry Show, Hip Poetry 2012, Ishaan Literary Review, Liquid Imagination, Manor House Quarterly, Open Road Review, Pirene's Fountain, Poecology, The Poet's Quest for God, Recours au Poème, Red Fez, Redheaded Stepchild, Southern Humanities Review, Tiferet Journal, Toronto Quarterly, Tryst, Tupelo Quarterly, Vox Poetica,* and *Your Daily Poem.*

I would also like to thank Amy King and Lois P. Jones for their generous manuscript insights, RJ Jeffreys for his consistent support and attention to individual poems, and Ron Starbuck for his many kindnesses and great patience as my publisher.

ABOUT THE AUTHOR

Melissa Studdard is the author the bestselling novel, *Six Weeks to Yehidah,* and other books. Her works have received numerous awards, including the Forward National Literature Award and the International Book Award. Her poems and short writings have appeared in dozens of journals and anthologies, and she serves or has recently served as a reviewer-at-large for *The National Poetry Review,* an interviewer for *American Microreviews and Interviews,* a professor for Lone Star College System, a teaching artist for The Rooster Moans Poetry Cooperative, an editorial adviser for *The Criterion,* and host of *Tiferet Talk* radio.

Learn more at, www.melissastuddard.com.

CPSIA information can be obtained at www.ICGtesting.com
Printed in the USA
LVOW11*1742210914

405133LV00002B/8/P